Catharsis

Katarina Rivers

Presentation by *BookLeaf Publishing*

Web: www.bookleafpub.com

E-mail: info@bookleafpub.com

ISBN: 9789358369786

First edition 2023

To my husband, Anthony- I am eternally grateful for you and your authentic, healthy love. I don't know where I would be without you. You helped me learn to heal myself and you stood beside me through it all, even the most difficult parts. You are my constant.

Worth It

Sometimes healing is a workbook
Sometimes its crying on the floor of the shower
at 3am.
Its throwing the pills out before its too late
Or checking yourself into the hospital
Because you don't trust that you'll be able to stop
yourself from giving in.
Sometimes in the singing off key in the car
To a song you never thought you could listen to
again
Because it was playing the night you were raped
at a party.
Its weekly therapy sessions,
Hugs thats feel like they last for what seems like
hours.
Sometimes its police reports and a victim impact
letter.
Its always messy
Always exhausting
But always worth it.

The Splintering Year

This was the "Almost Worst" year
The year 8-10 people squeezed into a rundown,
roach infested two bedroom trailer.
The year the drugs worse,
So much worse.
And my mother's newest abusive boyfriend
sauntered in.
This was the year food stamps and SSI saved us.

The year the new boyfriend threw a hammer at
my sister,
While my mother was in jail briefly.
Afterwards, my sister tried to overdose,
And I had to break the door down.
The year the boyfriend would watch me in the
bathroom,
The year I began to truly hate my body.
The year I slept on a pull out sofa with my three
brothers in the living room.
The year the bullying at school got worse.
The year I started drinking and smoking,
The year I decided I didn't want to live anymore
But I couldn't leave the world and let my
brothers suffer alone.

The year I had to hide my books, my art, my
music
Because the newest boyfriend read my diary
And tried to play loving step-father
Right after he asked me to look out for
undercover police
While he and my mother locked themselves in
their room
To lose themselves in meth.
The year I learned that not even my private
thoughts were safe.
I lived on eggshells,
Choked on my fears
But could not let it out.
Needed to put on a brave face
For my brothers and try to shield them as much
as I could.
This was the splintering year.

The Breaking Year

This was the worst year.
The year the foundation crumpled.
The year it finally happened:
A new step-dad
More drugs
More hurt
But at least we had a house.
I had a bedroom-
It used to be a back porch
So it wasn't insulated.
I had a small pallet on the floor and a ratty
pillow.
It was always cold and it was small
But it was mine.
This was the year I actually made good friends.
The year someone noticed me, my 8th grade
English teacher-
She saw the bruises, the baggy sweaters, the
meekness
And the spark that hadn't quite been snuffed out
But was definitely fading.
I used to take herbal tea and coffee to her class
An hour before the bell rang.
She would bring breakfast for us
Sometimes we would talk.

Other times we just read our books in silence.
It was peaceful and it was nice to know someone
cared.
Someone saw me.
She called social services after a while
But I wasn't angry by this,
I understood why.
She wanted to help me, to save me.
Social services showed up at my house shortly
after-
My mother told my sister, my brothers, and I to
pack a bag.
Curtis only packed toy trucks.
Turns out they didn't want to take us-
They wanted to monitor us
(I will never understand why they didn't take use
them.)
This was the year my mother tried to kill herself
in front of me
Over and over.
The year I busted down a bathroom door to stop
her.
The year I stuck my fingers down her throat
when she overdosed on anti-psychotics.
The year I became an expert in basic first aid,
Learned to stop the bleeding, bandage her wrists
and her neck.
I mopped io the blood and buried all of the
knives underneath the front porch.

This was the year my mother's boyfriend jumped
on my sister
And I tackled him, all 80lbs of me, like a rabid
animal.
The year he choked me until I began to lose
consciousness.
Because I wouldn't let him hit my brother
Riddock for playing too loudly.
I'll never forget his face, his eye, the way he
bared his teeth,
Not an ounce of remorse even after I thrashed
and kicked him
Until he finally let go of me.
The year my mother threw his weed into the
yard
So he hit her again
And again.
The cops came and as they were taking
statements
My best friends and their mom pulled up
To take me to see a movie with them.
They asked me if we should stay to help,
I said no, just drive away.
He has ran off so the danger wasn't imminent.
This was just a typical Saturday.
I wanted to ask them to just drive and never
come back
But I couldn't.
I had to come back

For my brothers.
They needed someone sober
To wake them up for school, to feed them, to
play games with them, to read them bedtime
stories, to sing them to sleep, and to hold them
when they were scared or sad.
Eventually my mother went to jail again.
At the time I didn't know it
But my sister made the hardest decision she ever
made-
A decision that saved us.
This was the breaking year.

Swallow

Tonight
My newest 'wellness counselor'
Asked me
"Aren't you angry about all the horrible things
that have been done to you?"
I swallowed the lump in my throat, preparing an
answer that seemed fitting
"Well, yeah, of course."
But I couldn't quite find the rest of the words,
Couldn't quite translate the thoughts swirling
inside of me.
I think I may have found them now though-
I've been holding onto hot coals
And swallowing a bitter poison.
Fighting with a thorn in my side, dagger in hand.
Blood pooling in my mouth, saturating my lips,
From biting my tongue for so long.
And I have been doing this for so long
For what feels like an eternity- barely surviving
That I didn't have much time or room for anger.
Now,
I am just so exhausted
So worn down.
I am just trying to tend my wounds,
Trying to ignore the battlefield of scars

That litters my body.
Anger feels like another war to come-
But I'm not sure if I can endure another battle;
But yes, I am angry- it lies beneath my surface,
Threatening to swallow me whole
Every single day.

Survive

Today I feel like giving up
But I won't.
I need to see my sister again
And hug her so tight that we can't breathe
And see my niece and nephews.
I need to see my children grow
Graduate, make their own families.
I need to grow old with my husband
And explore our world together,
Falling more and more in love with each other.
I need to see my friends again and show them
how much I care about them.
So today I feel like giving up
But I won't.
Because I have so much to see
And so much to do.
I have so much to live for.
So I will push through this day
And I will survive.

Salvation

He claimed to be a holy man,
A family man, dedicated father and devoted
husband.
A business man,
A man who cared about helping people.
Prayed day and night,
Read his holy book,
Attended bible study and stood in the front
pews,
Even got married in his church.

But that night
There was nothing holy or sacred about
What he did to me.

He drank beyond excess,
Smoked my cigarettes.
He told me that he knew it was wrong
But he wanted to touch me.
When I tried to leave, even reminded him his
wife would be home soon,
He grabbed me, fingers digging into my ribs,
Shoved me face down,
And ripped through my insides,
Claiming what wasn't his.

Leaving his mark on me,
Inside and out.
"No", "Don't", and "Please stop"
All fell on deaf ears.
When it was over,
I ran to the other side of the room,
Where the door to my room was,
He looked at me and he said
"I'm sorry".
I couldn't say I forgave him then.
I still can't now.

He can repent to his god and beg for redemption,
But nothing will repair what he broke,
And salvation is not coming from my lips.

Remains

Every one who has ever touched me
Without my consent
Took a piece of me with them
After they'd gotten what they wanted
And were done with me.

I don't know how much of me is even left of me
anymore.

Proof

I was frequently starving as a child,
Not just for food.
But for love.
I hunted for it between upturned couch cushions.
Sticky fingers looking for it like loose change,
Between the cigar wrappers, old beer cans,
empty baggies, and smashed meth pipes.
I never could quite find the love I craved
At home with my mother, trapped in her
addiction.
Instead I reached for it outside.
I hugged a feral cat once.
It clawed my face in its panic
But it didn't phase me one bit.
I was used to equating pain with all touch.
All through school I interlaced my fingers
With my friends'.
And I held onto them like my most prized
possession.
Their returned grips were tangible proof that
Someone, somewhere
Wanted to hold onto me too.

One and the Same

I have so much hurt inside me.
I pushed it down,
Further and further.
Packed it up tightly
Until I couldn't see it,
Out of sight, out of mind.
Until I couldn't feel it
On the back of my tongue
Threatening to spill from my mouth,
Through clenched teeth.

It's still there
But it's fossilized.
A dreary artifact
A testament to both
Survival and silence.
The edges of it are crumbling;
Jagged pieces.
I can no longer just push it down
Or hide it away.
It rips through my flesh and tendons,
A scream finally erupting.
Which is worse-
Reliving the pain

Or opening up old wounds?

Aren't they one and the same?

Never Mine

Last night was hard
Today is harder.
I made the foolish mistake
Of trying to drink away that memory.
It only made it more clear-
You sat across from me smiling.
The way you took something away from me that
night,
And how I am scared I will never recover it.
How you grabbed me and left bruises on my ribs
that didn't disappear for weeks after,
How you shoved my face down into the couch
cushion even as I told you-
Begged you
To stop.
How it all happened on that couch,
And how I hate even looking at it now,
I couldn't bring myself to sit on it afterwards.
How I remember the exact episode Jessica Jones
that was playing on the living room TV,
How you smelled like Natty Daddy's, cigarettes,
and sweat.
How I stumbled to the doorway to the
downstairs guest room I was staying in-
I turned to look at you-

Not wanting to believe this was happening.
How you looked at me with sad eyes,
Shame flooding your face,
How you said you were sorry.
(How dare you.)
How I went into the room silently,
Putting a chair under the door handle into the
room, moved a nightstand in front of the one
leading to the backyard, and moved the desk in
front of the door leading to the front yard.
Because you knew the code to all the door locks.
There was no room for misunderstanding-
I fervently said no, stood up and tried to leave
the room, told you your wife would be back
from ubering soon,
How you didn't care
And you didn't stop.
I can't comprehend how you could do that to me.
I had begun to look at you as a father figure,
Had learned to trust you,
How we got along so well.
But now, I am so scared of you
And scared of it happening again,
Or being blamed for it.
I haven't been able to stop thinking about you
Or that night.
The flashbacks and nightmares have persisted
since.

The intrusive thoughts play over and over in
mind,
Like a broken record.
How I still blame myself for it.
I keep going over what-ifs;
What if I went to bed early?
What if I didn't drink with you?
What if I was bigger or stronger or faster?
Just enough to get away.
Just enough to save myself for once.
The guilt and shame of this are so heavy-
Dragging me down.
It feels like there is a lead weight on my chest
And I can't even breathe.
Every single moment of every single day.
I want to lay this hurt
At your feet
To make you look at it,
To make you truly witness and comprehend
what you did to me.
To make you carry this burden
Because despite what my brain is telling me
I know that this is your guilt and shame to carry,
Not mine.
It has never been mine.

Mother

Today I miss my mother
Well, not her
But who she could and should be
If she would just try.
I want to call her
And tell her
They caught the man who raped me in 2011,
That I got a new job I really love,
That I miscarried again,
That her granddaughter is about to graduate
from elementary school,
That her grandson has been seizure free for a full
year.
I want to share the good and the bad with her
But I can't.
And that hurts.
Because I have always wanted her
To give up the drugs,
To take her medications,
To get stabilized,
To choose
Just once.
I want her to genuinely apologize to me
For all she's done
And all that she hasn't done.

But more than anything
I want to know what it feels like
To have a safe, loving mom
Instead of just a mother.

Life Skills

You never taught me how to cook or clean,
You never taught me about my body-
How to properly wash my hair, how to detangle
it.
How to shave or clean my face to prevent acne.
You never taught me what a period was,
Never talked to me about consent
Or what to do when it was stolen.
You never taught me about safe sex.
I learned these things on my own,
Often in the worst ways possible.

Instead
You taught me how to hide a baggie of meth in
the lining of a bra,
How to cook heroin with limited resources,
How to identify undercover cops and unmarked
police cars,
What liquor gets you the drunkest quickest,
And how to temporarily drown your demons
with it.
You taught me how to melt down-
How to open a vein, to bleed out your pain,
How to clean up a crime scene,

How to get bloodstains out of your clothing, out
of your furniture and out of the grout.
How to lie to everyone,
How to swallow fists, broken teeth, and bitter
blood.
How to run, how to fight dirty, to hide and
cower.
You taught me how to survive
Because god knows I needed to,
Living with you.

Kept

Growing up
Home was a foreign concept.
Hard to find a home
When you move 20+ times a year.
Then came foster care
A series of houses
A series of fake families
Houseparents at group homes
Who tried to love me
Through actions and words
Sneaking me coffee and cups of Dr. Pepper
(I love you Ms. Lynn)
But home was still foreign

But then
I met him
A boy with black and silver hair
Carrying my bags in
An Inuyasha backpack
A 100 watt smile
A kiss on my calloused hands
A month of butterflies
And kisses snuck behind
The backs of group home staff
My heart

It sang for him
Then he had to go
And my heart felt homeless

More than the year I lived with
My mother and my sister in a beaten down car.
More than that month in a hotel
More than the year of sleeping
In emergency shelters
More than the years in too small trailers
With 'family' I barely knew.

My heart had found its new home
And it would not settle for anything less
Even when my brain told me it was hopeless.

But then a miracle
A kind caseworker sneaking letters
Secret phone calls and MySpace messages
And a promise to never let go.
He kept me.

Today

Today is the first day
I didn't wake up with your name
Straddling my bloody and chapped lips.
The first day my tongue wasn't raw
From biting back screams.
The word rape digests like snakes,
Writhing inside me
But I don't feel it taking place today.
Today I can look in the mirror
Into my own eyes
And say "I love you. It wasn't your fault."
And actually believe it.
I can label what you did to me as wrong
And know I didn't deserve it.
I don't think you will ever comprehend
How much strength that takes.
Today feels a lot like healing.

Healing

This morning I woke up
With your name in my throat
Burning like acid.
I wanted to stay in bed and hide
But I got up.
I showered, washed your handprints away.
I brushed my teeth, rinsed you from my mouth.
I brushed my hair, detangled your fingers.
I dressed in a way I like.
I texted my sister, my lifeline.
I read a book of poetry.
Sipped on coffee and smoked you out.
I know today is hard,
I know tomorrow might be too.
But I'm still here
So I fight your memory with bloodied knuckles.
This is messy, this is painful.
This is healing.

Happily Ever After

Growing up
I learned
To do everything in my power
To banish the negative energy around me.
I grew up with names carved into black candles,
The flame purifying the soul,
The wax signifying the darkness seeping out.
Raised
With superstitions as my gospel.
Lift your feet when you go over a bridge so the
bridge doesn't collapse,
Throw salt over your shoulder after you spill it
to banish bad luck.
When you drop a dishrag, shake it out to ward
off unwelcome and unexpected guests.
Don't do laundry on New Years Day, lest you
wash a loved one away.
Don't allow anyone to sweep your feet; if you do
then you'll never get married:

The funny thing is that as a child I begged
everyone to sweep my feet.
I didn't want to marry because all I knew of love
Was the wounds it left and the way it twisted
people into creatures unknown.

The manipulation of it,
The guilt of it.
All marriage seemed to be was a piece of paper,
Something tenuous and shaky at best.

As I grew, I became more guarded.
Compounded by complex trauma,
A war cry brewing in my throat,
A fire alight in my womb.
White knuckles, bitten tongues, and narrowed
eyes.
I spit venom,
Swallowed poison,
And held the hot coals of hatred in my palms.
Told myself I didn't need or want anyone else.
That I was content with the hollowness in my
heart,
The weight on my chest.
With the loneliness
In my bones.
I became vicious,
Bared teeth, extended talons, a snarl ripping
through the air.
I was fooling not only the world but myself as
well.

Then you came along-
I tried to ignore the race of my pulse when you
said my name.

The way I lost my breath when you looked me
in the eyes.
Tried to ignore the fluttering in my stomach
when you smiled at me.

I may have been hiding
But you found me.
You saw through the armor,
Saw through the angry girl-
All the way, straight to the one who was lost and
too scared to allow herself to feel anything.
The one buried beneath the rubble of her past.
And you breathed life into her.

Your words written on my forearm,
Stolen kisses in the van or on the picnic tables
outside.
Hand written letters passed back and forth-
It all started to change me.

With my hand in yours,
For the very first time,
I felt safe.
Wrapped in your arms,
I finally felt something that felt like home.
It felt like something that I could lean on,
Something that wouldn't slip through my
fingers.
It felt real.

And when they tried to take you away,
We held each other tightly as we cried,
Every cell in my body begging me to not let go
of you.
Every single piece of my body cried out for you.
And when you had to leave,
It felt like a piece of me was ripped out the
moment the car you were in disappeared.
It was an ache that I still cannot describe,
It was earth shattering.
Every breath was difficult,
As if when they took you,
They took the one thing that was keeping me
alive.
But I held on for dear life,
Because I couldn't lose you.
And much to my surprise,
You held on, too.
I was still scared,
But I knew that you,
You were someone worth holding onto,
For as long as you would allow me to.

They never gave me the letters you sent,
They wouldn't tell me where you were
Or why you were forced to leave.
But even not knowing that you were still trying
to reach for me,

I kept waiting.
Because I couldn't imagine doing anything else.
How could I do anything else-
You had become the brightest star in my sky
And I loved the view.
Suddenly you were able to call,
Using a different name, of course,
Because they were hell-bent on tearing us apart.
And when you were able to come to town,
We snuck around to see each other.
Holding onto each other so tightly again,
I was surprised we didn't turn to dust in each
others embrace.
I caused you to be late meeting with your uncle
But you assured me it was worth it.
When I went back to HH,
I was euphoric,
So stunned and grateful
For your existence.

We managed to keep fighting tooth and nail
For each other,
For the love we had found
In a place we least expected it.
We didn't let them destroy us and
I didn't let them take away the best thing that
ever happened to me.

And I can't say it was always easy because some
days were hard and heart-wrenching-
But through all of the messiness
In my brain,
You stayed by side.
Through the future heartaches and the loss,
You let me lean on you,
Let me cry into your shoulder,
Lie in your lap while you stroked my hair and
rubbed circles into my back while I sobbed.
You let me talk about all of the things that had
turned me to stone and you didn't flinch-
You simply listened and that was all I needed, I
realized.
Just someone to listen and believe me.
Someone who still loved me after hearing all of
it.
I expected you to run for the hills honestly-
Instead, you held me like I was the most
precious gift you'd ever received.

You built me up every time I tore myself down.
You fought for me
When I was ready to throw in the towel
And wave the white flag.
You were the very first person to not give up on
me.
The first person who told me I was strong.
The first person to believe in me.

The first person to love me unconditionally,
And the one who showed me what love really
was-
What it should and could be.

You saw through the self-sabotage,
Saw through the self-inflicted damage.
Saw past the scars.
You saw through the symptoms and instead saw
me-
Not my illness.
You helped me fight to begin healing,
Walking that long road with me.
And on the days where my legs were weak,
You carried me down the path,
Reminding me that I would be okay,
That you were there
And I was safe,
And that we could face anything together.

And we have-
We've faced so much-
Battled so many demons,
Fought so many wars,
Screamed until we lost our voices,
And we made it.
We are here,
14 years later.
We made each other stronger-

We held each other up-
We built this life together
Despite how we were raised,
Despite the poor examples set forth for us from
our family.
We broke the cycle-
We created our own destiny,
Wrote our own love story,
Changed the ending
To what we needed,
All the while knowing that
'Happily Ever After' is just the beginning.

Handle

I don't know how to love gently
Love has only ever been a war.
And I've been wounded on that battlefield so
many times
That I have become accustomed to the feeling
Of a blade in my back
And blood on my hands.
Venom coating my lips
I would love to lay my sword and shield down
But I am terrified
Of being deceived again,
Or worse yet, broken again.
Of losing this everlasting battle.
I trust in the security of fighting
More than the unknown perils of war
And what comes after.

I'm afraid that once I open up
I'll never be able to suture myself closed.
Worried that if I try to let out even a few tears,
The dam I've built will burst.
Afraid that my love
Might be more deadly than fragile.
Scared that if I let anyone see
The mess inside of me,

They'll decide that
It's too much to handle,
That I am too much to handle.

Growth

I'm a child,
Born of two addicts.
Stemming from a family tree,
Littered with empty Whiskey bottles.
Crawling with ghosts and generational trauma.
I am what happens
When one disaster collides with another.
I am a product of late nights spent in dirty
trailers,
Scattered with beer bottles, overflowing
ashtrays, crack pipes, lines of coke, and baggies
of meth.
I am the daughter of tragedy, passed down from
generation to generation.
An ode to the long-forgotten promises my
parents made,
The ones where they swore,
They'd never repeat their parents mistakes.
I am a byproduct of family secrets and family
shame.
I am a daughter,
I am a granddaughter,
Yet some of these familial connections
Are still shrouded.

Because who can keep track of paternity and
family records in tattered bibles,
When they're so high they can barely remember
their names?

I am a sister,
Sister to a goddess,
Born of a different father,
But he's probably not too different from my
own,
Other than his skin.
I am sister,
To a walking miracle,
A protector and best friend,
One who fought off monsters in the dark,
Before we knew them to be just men.
Just men,
As if man is not the most dangerous threat to
itself.
As if acknowledging the being
Makes it less volatile.

Now though,
Now I am mother-
Mother to amazing children,
Raised on love, not survival.
And they are picking flowers, not battles.
They play hide and seek,
The actual game-

Not the way I tried to hide my entire childhood.
They are loud and rowdy and sometimes drive
me crazy-
But they are happy, they are healthy-
And they feel safe enough to be themselves-
Even when they may be aggravating at times,
They know they are loved and that they will
always have their mother to turn to.

I have gone from seed to sapling to flower-
I started out in the dirt, crawling with bugs and
saturated with feces.
I managed to burst out of my shell,
Reach towards the light,
Towards something more,
Something better.
And by God, I found it.
Or it found me.

Genetics

I hate that I have your eyes
Your bone structure
Your accent
Your colorful euphemisms.

I hate that I have the same handwriting
Because every time I write,
And I write a lot,
I think of you
With every penstroke.

How can I ever truly be free of you
And what you did to me
When I see you every day
In the mirror
And when I hear you
Every time I open my mouth to speak?

From Me

He talked about my tattoo during my assault,
How he said I was a gift,
He said he loved my piercings.

Now all I want to do
Is to rip the piercings out,
To scrub the tattoo off,
And shower in scalding hot water
Until I no longer feel him holding me down.

But I won't.
I already threw out the dress and underwear
I was wearing the night it happened.
Buried them in the trash can,
Under empty beer cans and paper plates.
I didn't wear another dress for 3 months.
I stopped wearing my hair down when it was
curly for a year,
After he said he liked my natural curls.

He will not take anything else from me.

Everything

When a man you've come to see as father figure
Leaves bruises on your ribs, on your hips
In the shape of his fingerprints,
From when he pinned you down,
Your screams muffled by couch cushions,
It alters you.
Something inside you just breaks.

But the changes are hardly consistent;
One day you are hellfire-
Fueled by rage
Wanting to light him up
Until nothing of him remains
Except ash and memories.

Other days
You are a torrential downpour;
Decimated debris surrounding you,
Floods pouring down your cheeks,
You feel more broken than beautiful.

Some days you are all fear, defenses up:
A coiled serpent, venom dripping from a
copper-tasting mouth-
Ready to strike at anyone

Who ever touches you again.

And many days,
You are numb;
Present physically but a million miles away
Mentally and emotionally.
Simply a shell,
Just going through the motions to survive.

This is to say that this betrayal, this violation,
It seeps into everything you've ever known
And it changes everything-
Including yourself.